ICELANDIC
FOLK LEGENDS

ALDA SIGMUNDSDÓTTIR

ICELANDIC
FOLK LEGENDS

LITTLE BOOKS
PUBLISHING

TABLE OF CONTENTS

Introduction

One evening, many years ago, I was travelling through south Iceland with two of my cousins. We stopped in the town of Vík to camp for the night. After pitching our tent at the campsite we decided to take a walk before turning in. It was in the middle of summer, so it was broad daylight even though it was late in the evening.

After a short stroll we came to a place where we had a gorgeous black sand beach on our right, a grassy area (on which we were walking) in the middle, and a steep mountainside on our left. The waves were rolling in, and on the beach was a large colony of arctic terns. As many readers will know, arctic terns are exceedingly aggressive birds, and as we passed, literally hundreds, if not thousands, of them flew up screeching and shrieking, instantly starting to dive-bomb our heads in an effort to drive us away.

Suddenly we stopped dead in our tracks. Through the screeching of the birds we heard this incredible sound, like a huge banquet going on, with hundreds of people laughing and talking, glasses clinking, dinnerware clanking … all coming from somewhere beyond the cliffs. We looked at each other, completely mystified. Where was that sound coming from? Was it from the campsite? We decided it couldn't be – we'd only just left it and the number of people required to make that sound, not to mention all those glasses and dinnerware, could not possibly have been transported there in such a short time. Was it from the town? Hardly – the sound seemed like it was just beyond our line of vision and the town was too far away. Was there a banquet hall around, somewhere? Perhaps back from where we had come? We certainly couldn't rule it out, even though none of us had seen one.

The strange thing was, the party sounded like it was inside the cliff, but we obviously knew it couldn't be. Or could it? We had pretty much ruled out all possibilities, and were starting to think Shakespeare had hit the nail on the head with the immortal words: "There are more things in heaven and earth, Horatio, than are dreamt of in your philosophy."

We stood there for about ten minutes. That is how long it took us to recognize that the sound was being made by the combination of the birds screeching and the waves rolling in, echoing off the cliffs to our left. At that moment we realized that this was the sort of fantastical experience that must have made our ancestors conclude that trolls lived inside the mountains. How could they possibly have come to any other conclusion?

We mused on this a while as we continued our trek. We thought about all those formations rising out of the lava fields that seemed to move in the mist or twilight. Or dark shapes on the rims of the mountains, which appeared to be alive in the fading light when silhouetted against the sky. And what about the howls of the wind in the midwinter nights? Surely it was not too much of a stretch to believe those were the voices of the dead – particularly if the presence of ghosts was a normal part of life for you.

Suddenly it became clear how natural phenomena such as these could become transformed into stories that people told each other. After all, stories were what kept the spirit of the Icelandic nation alive in those long, harsh, oppressive winters, when people were forced to spend most of their time indoors. With wood virtually nonexistent, the Icelanders made their houses mostly out of rocks and turf. There was hardly any light or ventilation, since anything that allowed for such comfort also released precious warmth. All the members of a household, which typically included the farmer and his family, various farmhands, and sometimes orphans or widows who had been allocated a place at the farm, lived together in communal quarters called the *baðstofa*. The word baðstofa literally means "bath chamber" and at the time of the settlement it was used for the room in the house where people bathed. However, as the Icelanders gradually stripped the land of its abundant forests and firewood became scarce, people were forced closer and closer together in an effort to stay warm. Eventually, all the members of a household occupied the baðstofa, which was only around six or seven ells wide (just under four meters, or about thirteen feet) and was often built above the sheep shed to utilize the warmth from the animals. There were beds along both walls and a narrow aisle in the middle, and this was where people lived, slept, ate and carried out their winter tasks – working the wool, knitting and weaving, making shoes, clothing and tools, preserving food … essentially all the tasks that required working with the hands and could be performed indoors. Those tasks were reserved for the winter, of course, since the summer, with its precious light and more accommodating climate, was used for outdoor work.

From our twenty-first-century perspective, it is hard to fathom that people could exist in such conditions – and stay sane. Imagine living in such close proximity to other people, in houses that were dank, musty, and filled with bugs. Washing was considered unnecessary and hygiene was non-existent. People smelled, chamber pots smelled, the fish oil used for the lamps smelled, and the animals beneath the floor smelled. The bedding was cleaned only once a year, in the spring, when it was taken out and washed in urine, then rinsed in a brook and laid out on shrubs to dry. Similarly, the floors were cleaned only once a year, when debris and other matter that had formed a thick cake-like substance on the floorboards was scraped off and dumped outside.

Yet, people survived. Not only did they feed their bodies, but they managed to feed their minds and spirits as well. The Icelanders at this time forged a standard of literacy that was among the highest in the world. Despite their abject poverty, virtually everyone in the country could read and write, people were remarkably well informed about history and geography, and they read daily from the Scriptures. All of this was primarily due to one widespread custom that was effectively a national institution: the *kvöldvaka*.

The word kvöldvaka is a compound noun: *kvöld* meaning "evening" and *vaka* essentially meaning "staying awake." Basically this was the term used for the indoor activity that people undertook in the evenings, and which consisted mostly of storytelling. It was done to pass the time while they sat on their beds and carried out whatever winter tasks they had been allocated. Their stories consisted of folk tales, like the ones that you will read in this book, stories of heroic exploits (sometimes their own, sometimes those of others), re-tellings of the Icelandic Sagas, epic poetry recited in a sort of singsong fashion (called *að ríma* in Icelandic), or gossip from the neighboring farms. Indeed, there was a whole subculture of vagrants who moved from one farm to another, whose "job" it was to pass news (or gossip!) from place to place. They stayed at different farms for longer or shorter periods, and many of them were considered a nuisance – but not those who were good storytellers. They were almost always welcome. Some of them even stockpiled books that they carried around with them, stuffed inside their outer clothing, which was then bound with string around the waist to prevent the books from falling out the bottom.

The kvöldvaka was also where children were taught to read and write, and as such it played a hugely significant role in creating the abovementioned standard of literacy.

In almost all cases, the kvöldvaka ended with the so-called *húslestur*, literally the "house reading," which consisted of someone, usually the master of the house, reading from the Scriptures. While the húslestur was being performed, everyone stopped what they were doing to listen, or at least engaged only in quiet activities, such as knitting. The húslestur generally began and ended with a hymn where everyone joined in, and when the reading was finished, the members of the house-hold thanked the reader by saying *þökk fyrir les-turinn*, or "thank you for the reading." After that, everyone retired. The húslestur is mentioned in a couple of tales in this book as part of the religious motif that runs through the stories like a red thread in a tapestry.

Personally I find the strong role that Christianity and religion plays in the Icelandic folk stories fasci-nating, particularly since the nation is so very secular today (confirmations and religious holidays notwith-standing). Most of the apparitions and supernatural beings that feature in the stories represent the antith-esis of Christian values, and as such are to be feared and shunned. Some of them, like the elves and hid-den people, would try to tempt mortals to leave their Christian ways and to join them – something that was considered a mortal sin and would surely lead to ruin. As such they served as morality tales, as much as stories for people's entertainment.

Today, television and computers have replaced the kvöldvaka, and science has helped debunk the beliefs that in the past were attributed to mystic beings, spir-its, and other apparitions. It is a new era ... and yet, Icelandic folk legends remain very much alive in the psyche of the Icelandic people. Not in the sense that we take them literally or speak about them daily – I don't know of anyone who would, for example, talk about the elf family that lives in the boulder next door, as though they were a normal part of life (in spite of what the foreign media, or tourist marketing people, would have you believe). Yet if that same someone was out on a hike with a friend and passed by a particularly imposing boulder, they might remark on the "impressive elf-stone" or similar.

That being said, as I write this I am reminded that the Icelandic psyche is fraught with paradox. Consequently it is my duty to say that modern Icelanders *have* been known to divert roads past boulders that people have claimed were elf rocks. In fact, not too long ago an Icelandic MP had a boulder transported by ferry from the mainland to his home in the Westman Islands, and actually paid a fare for the "elf couple" that was supposedly being moved along with the rock. Given the media coverage this received, not to mention this particular MP's somewhat, ehh, *colorful* track record (he did time for extortion, which he committed while in office) I hope you will forgive me for doubting the sincerity of his actions, and to ascribe this particular exercise to a striving for attention rather than a genuine concern for the poor, uprooted elf couple.

Another example of an old legend finding its way into our lives today is in the story of the hideous ogress Grýla, with which just about every man, woman and child in Iceland is intimately acquainted.

Grýla, you see, eats naughty children, and Icelandic parents, desperately concerned for their children's safety, warn them about this *early*. According to lore, Grýla lives in a cave and has a habit of coming into residential areas for the express purpose of stuffing disobedient kiddies into her sack, carrying them back to her cave and throwing them into a large cauldron of boiling water she perpetually has on the fire. Curiously, though, Grýla does not appear to have a taste for her own offspring. She is the mother of the thirteen Icelandic Yule Lads, who happen to be renowned for their naughtiness – yet there are no reports of her having eaten any of them.

I suppose what I'm trying to say is, while we no longer take our folk legends literally, they are nevertheless part of the glue that holds the Icelandic nation together. They are a common heritage, a cultural point of reference that every Icelander can relate to. They give us an identity, and make us feel like we belong to something larger than ourselves.

Some of these stories will no doubt seem vaguely familiar to many readers, in particular "Gilitrutt" and "The Church Builder," both of which bear a strong resemblance to the well-known "Rumpelstiltskin." That is because folk legends tended to migrate, taking on the special characteristics and features of the different areas where they took root (what the eminent ethnologist Carl Wilhelm von Sydow termed oicotype). Many Icelandic folk legends are therefore the Icelandic oicotypes of various known legends.

Interestingly, there is one particular motif in Icelandic folk tales that is unique to Iceland. I'm sure we are all familiar with the bad stepmother (or stepfather) motif – but in Iceland, we have the motif of the *good* stepmother, which apparently is not found in folk tales elsewhere. Mind you, I have not done any extensive research on this, but have it directly from the mouth of one of my university folkloristics professors, and I would hope she knows what she is talking about.

I have been asked why I chose the particular stories that appear in this collection. Full disclosure: I didn't. My translations of these tales originally appeared in print in 1998, and the publisher at the time was the one who selected them. I can surmise that at least some of them were chosen for their popularity – "The Deacon of Myrká," for example, is probably the best-known Icelandic ghost story. Others stories present themes or motifs that surface in many different Icelandic folk legends, such as the wrath of the hidden people when mortals refuse their requests for help ("The Hidden Woman's Curse"), or the hidden valleys beyond the mountains where mysterious outlaws reside in relative affluence ("The Vanished Bride").

In this edition I have added this introduction and the subsequent "field guide," plus three more stories that were not in the original publication: "Gilitrutt," "Búkolla," and "The Story of Himinbjörg." I chose the first two because they are well known and well loved, and because my grandmother told them to me when I was little. The last I chose because it features the aforementioned motif of the good stepmother.

In the interests of accuracy, I should probably add a proviso: despite the title of this book, not all of these stories are legends. Many of them fall into the category of folk tales, and some, like "The Story of Himinbjörg," are more akin to fairy tales. Rest assured, though, that they are all very much a part of Iceland's cultural legacy.

A few words about the style. Since the stories were originally passed down verbally and subsequently written down, they tend to be in a very terse, clipped format that presented a bit of a challenge in the translation. It is a little difficult to capture the right tone in such cases, while still getting across the pulsing heart of the narrative. To some, the stories may seem brusque or harsh, but that is only because in the verbal telling they were stripped of any ornamentation. What you get are the bare bones. Some of them may also seem disjointed and strange – particularly the story "Þorgeir's Bull," which can only be described as extraordinarily weird. I have even wondered sometimes if the people who made up that story were *on* something. I mentioned this to my husband, who told me that reports exist about rotten flour or meal having been imported to Iceland, and when people ate it, they started hallucinating. I can't help but think that this might apply to that story.

And while I'm on the subject of "Þorgeir's Bull," allow me to add a quick note: for the print edition of this book I have included the two Icelandic special characters Þ and Ð (or ð). They are pronounced, respectively, as a voiced "th" sound (as in "thistle") and a silent "th" sound (as in "there").

Finally, this introduction would not be complete without a few words about the preservation of the folk tales. In the mid-nineteenth century there was widespread nationalistic revival in Europe, which gave rise to a new interest in folk stories that had been passed on verbally. Interested parties began collecting such tales and writing them down, the best known undoubtedly being Jacob and Wilhelm Grimm in Germany, whose efforts resulted in the renowned *Grimm's Fairy Tales*. In Iceland, a similar undertaking was initially launched by two men: Jón Árnason, a scholar and later Iceland's national librarian, and Magnús Grímsson. They published a collection entitled *Íslenzk ævintýri* in 1852, which garnered a lukewarm reception, as folk stories were not considered significant or important by the general population at that time. A few years later, a German scholar named Konrad von Maurer travelled in Iceland and recorded stories, culminating in a published book in Leipzig in 1860 entitled *Isländische Volkssagen der Gegenwart*. He also assisted Árnason and Grímsson in having their collection of Icelandic folk stories published in Germany, where they appeared in two separate volumes between 1862 and 1864. Grímsson passed away in 1860, but Jón Árnason continued to record stories in succeeding years. It would be almost a century, however, before his full collection of Icelandic folk tales was published in six volumes, from 1954 to 1961. The stories in this book are taken from that six-volume collection, which today is commonly referred to as *Þjóðsögur Jóns Árnasonar*, or *The Folk Tales of Jón Árnason*.

APPARITIONS IN ICELANDIC FOLK TALES
A FIELD GUIDE

Ghosts

Ghosts in Icelandic folk stories tend to be malicious and spiteful creatures – nasty pieces of work that go after people for no particular reason. Some are conjured up by people who control them behind the scenes and make them perform evil deeds. Ghosts are not able to speak the word Guð, or God – useful to keep in mind when you are uncertain whether or not you are dealing with an apparition. (Just ask them politely if they could say "Guð" for you – if they can't then they are probably a ghost.) This is irrespective of whether it is the word Guð by itself, or as part of a compound word. For instance, in "The Deacon of Myrká," the ghost calls a woman named Guðrún "Garún" because he isn't able to say the first part of her name. Another feature of ghosts is that their supernatural powers seemed to become less potent over time, as in "Þorgeir's Bull," for example. Meaning that, if you can't get rid of the thing, your best bet may be to simply wait it out.

Outlaws

Outlaws figure prominently in Icelandic folk tales. They are actual mortals who have gone to live in the highlands, far from civilization. Some have been banished from society for committing a crime, whereas others have left voluntarily for whatever reason. Some outlaws live in caves, and most of them kill livestock for food. If farmers are missing sheep, it is usually the outlaws who are blamed. Folks tend to be a bit ambivalent when it comes to outlaws. They generally inspire fear and dread – but also a grudging respect for being able to survive in the Icelandic highlands. An interesting feature of outlaw stories is that, over time, the line between them and hidden people stories began to blur. For instance in the story "The Outlaw on Kiðuvallafjall Mountain," the outlaw lives in a boulder and winds up possessing a large fortune when he dies. In some stories, outlaws are depicted as living in remote locations with lush valleys where there are hot springs and pools for bathing. This is analogous to the way hidden people were believed to have homes filled with gold and riches, and to live in enchanted worlds, set apart from the drudgery of everyday life. An element of this may be found in "The Vanished Bride," where the farmer comes upon a farm in a remote location that no one seems to know about, where the master of the house has an abundance of livestock and lives a prosperous life. Indeed, the personages of that story are somewhat ambiguous, and appear to be some sort of merger between enchanted hidden people and outlaws who are in self-imposed exile from society.

Trolls and ogres

These beings, who are very large and live inside caves or mountains, are typically not very bright, which is both their strength and weakness. On the one hand, their sheer size, coupled with their stupidity, makes them dangerous. On the other hand, their stupidity means they are not clever or devious, so those unfortunate enough to be captured by them can usually escape by outwitting them. Trolls are often cannibals and like the taste of human flesh. The most horrific troll-slash-ogre in Icelandic mythology is the dreaded Grýla (we met her in the introduction), who for centuries (or at least decades) has been shamelessly used by parents to manipulate their offspring into behaving (as in, "If you're not good, Grýla will come get you!"). Incidentally, Grýla seems to be an Icelandic oicotype of a folk character designed to frighten children – a local version of the bogeyman. There are two types of trolls: the normal kind that goes about its business day or night, and the other kind that cannot bear daylight and turns to stone when the sun comes up. Those are the night trolls, and their petrified remains (read: stone pillars) may be found all over Iceland.

Elves and hidden people

These are certainly the most complex and beguiling apparitions in Icelandic folklore. They are variously called *álfar* (elves) or *huldufólk* (hidden people) but basically they are the same type of being. These elves have little in common with their diminutive counterparts in other countries. For one thing, they are not short, but tall and regal and a lot better looking than the sad, sniveling mortals around them. Their clothing tends to be opulent, made of fine fabrics with intricate embroidery. Their homes are often lavish, with sumptuous tapestries, plush upholstery and lots of silver and gold. They live inside boulders and hillocks, and are invisible to humans unless they choose to be seen. Frequently they appear and speak to people in dreams, and if they do, it is usually because they want something. If Icelandic folk legends are anything to go by, the hidden women experience distress in childbirth with alarming frequency, and mortal women are then called upon to help. If they comply, they are usually amply rewarded – for example, their fields might yield the best hay, or their rivers the largest fish. If, on the other hand, they refuse to help, they are almost sure to incur the everlasting wrath of the hidden people and experience great misfortune. In other words: *do not piss off the elves*.

Temptation figures highly in many hidden people stories. For instance, the most lush, verdant grass might grow on an elf hillock, but woe to anyone who dares touch it, for the homes of the hidden people are sacrosanct. You might be allowed to cut the grass anywhere else, even all around the hillock – but make sure you keep off the elf knoll. In some stories, the elves try to lure people into coming to live with them, and such offers can be exceedingly tempting because the lives of the hidden people are shrouded in mystery and glamour. Yet those who are able to resist their heathen ways are celebrated for their integrity and strength and are practically hailed as heroes. Curiously, there are quite a few stories of children being brought up by hidden people, and later returning to mortal society. Those people do not seem to have suffered at all from their upbringing – on the contrary, they normally go on to have successful, prosperous lives.

These are the apparitions found in this particular collection of tales. However, there are a handful of other beings that feature in Icelandic lore, including *skoffín* (offspring of a fox and a female cat), *skuggabaldur* (offspring of a tomcat and vixen [female fox] or bitch), *nykur* (water horse with hooves that face backwards), *margígur* (top half human, bottom half fish), and *marbendill* (top half dwarf, bottom half seal).

Gilitrutt

here once was a young farmer who lived beneath Eyjafjöll mountains in south Iceland. He was a dili-gent and industrious young man. The surrounding regions were considered good sheep-rearing country and the farmer owned many sheep. He was newly married when this story took place, to a young and idle woman. She was indifferent to the farm work and not motivated in the least. This upset the farmer, yet there was very little he could do.

One autumn the farmer brought his wife a large sack of wool and asked her to make it into cloth for the winter. Her response was decidedly apathetic. Winter came, and the farmer's young wife did not touch the wool, despite her husband's repeated urgings.

One day, an old crone of rather coarse build came to see the woman, to ask her for a favor.

"Can you do something for me in return?" asked the woman.

"Possibly," said the crone, "what sort of work would you have me do?"

"Fashioning wool into cloth," said the woman.

"Give it to me, then," said the crone.

The woman handed her the large sack of wool. The old crone took the sack, slung it across her back, and said: "I will bring you the cloth on the First Day of Summer."

"What will you take as your reward?" asked the woman.

"It will not be much," said the crone, "you must simply tell me my name on the third try, and we shall be even."

The woman agreed to this, and the crone left.

Winter wore on, and the farmer repeatedly asked his wife how the wool cloth was coming along. She replied that it was none of his concern, but that he should have it on the First Day of Summer. The farmer accepted this, and the end of winter approached. The woman then turned her thoughts to what the old crone's name might be, but saw no way of discovering it. She grew anxious and distressed. The farmer noticed the change in her and asked her what the matter was. At this, she confessed the whole story. The farmer became frightened and told her she had done a terrible deed, for the old crone was surely an ogress who planned to abduct her.

Some time later, the farmer was headed up the side of a nearby mountain when he arrived at a large, rocky knoll. He was deeply absorbed by his concerns and hardly knew where he was. Suddenly he heard a knocking coming from inside the knoll.

He followed the sound, and came to a crevice. Inside he saw an old woman of coarse build sitting at a loom, weaving excitedly. She repeated, over and over: "Ha ha, hee hee. Mistress does not know my name, ha ha, hee hee. Gilitrutt is my name, ha ha. Gilitrutt is my name, ha ha, hee hee." This she muttered again and again, working the loom with great speed. Seeing this, the farmer brightened, as he was quite sure that this was the old crone who had come to see his wife the previous autumn. He went home and wrote down the name Gilitrutt on a snippet of paper.

Now the last day of winter approached. The farmer's wife became deeply despondent and spent whole days in bed. The farmer went to her and asked if she knew the name of the crone who had done the wool work for her. She said that she did not and that she would now die of despair. The farmer replied that that would not be necessary, handed her the paper with the name on it, and told her the whole story. She took it, trembling with fear, for she was afraid that the name might be wrong. She asked the farmer to be by her side when the old crone came. He refused, saying: "You did not consult me when you gave her the wool, so it is best that you see her by yourself."

The First Day of Summer arrived and the woman lay alone in bed. No one else was at the farm. Suddenly she heard a great rumbling and the hideous old crone entered. She tossed a large roll of wool cloth onto the floor and demanded: "What is my name, then, what is my name?"

The young woman, nearly frightened out of her wits, replied: "Signý?"

"What is my name, what is my name: guess again, mistress!" said the crone.

"Ása?" the young woman stuttered.

The old crone replied: "What is my name, what is my name, guess yet again, mistress!"

"Your name wouldn't be ... Gilitrutt?" ventured the young woman.

At this the old crone received such a jolt that she fell headlong on the floor with a loud thud. She then got to her feet, left the place, and was never seen again.

The young woman was so relieved to have made this happy escape from the ogress that she became completely transformed. She turned industrious and organized, and always worked her own wool from then on.

Note: *The First Day of Summer according to the Old Icelandic Calendar is observed on a Thursday from April 19-25 in any given year. The old calendar had only two seasons, winter and summer. The First Day of Summer is still observed as a public holiday – a testament to the importance of summer for the Icelanders.*

The Deacon of
Myrká Church

I n former times there was a deacon who lived
at the farm Myrká in Eyjafjörður, north Iceland, which was also the site of the parish church.
His name is not known, but he is said to have been
involved with a woman named Guðrún. She was
employed as a maid by the parson at Bægisá, on the
opposite side of the Hörgá river. The deacon had
a grey-maned horse named Faxi, which he always
rode.

One winter, just before Christmas, the deacon rode
to Bægisá to invite Guðrún to Christmas festivities at
Myrká. A great deal of snow had fallen in the days
preceding his journey and patches of ice lay on the

ground. That particular day, however, there was a sudden thaw; the snow melted and conditions turned slushy and wet. As the day wore on, the river swelled and became impassable, with rushing ice floes and heavy rapids. The deacon, meanwhile, was unaware of the changing conditions during his visit to Bægisá. When he left for home he promised to fetch Guðrún at a pre-arranged time on Christmas Eve and escort her to the festivities.

The deacon was able to cross the Yxnadalsá river by an ice bridge, but when he arrived at Hörgá river he saw that it had cleared itself of ice. He rode along the riverbank until he was opposite Saurbær, one farm removed from Myrká, where he found an ice bridge still whole. He urged his horse onto it, but when he reached the center the bridge collapsed and man and horse fell into the rapids.

The following morning when the farmer at Þúfna-vellir, next to Saurbær, got up, he could see a saddled horse at the far end of his hayfield. This horse, he thought, bore a close resemblance to the deacon's Faxi and he found this disquieting for the previous day he had seen the deacon ride past, but had not noticed him return. Thus he suspected the worst. He hastened over to the end of his hayfield and saw that it was indeed Faxi, all wet and battered. The farmer then went down to the river where he came upon the deacon's corpse, lying at the edge of a small peninsula called Þúfnavallanes. The back of the head was badly mutilated, presumably having collided with an ice floe. The farmer immediately went over to Myrká to report the news. The deacon's body was then taken there and was buried sometime in the week before Christmas.

No news of the incident reached Bægisá while the adverse conditions prevailed. On Christmas Eve day the weather improved considerably and Guðrún was very much looking forward to the Myrká festivities. She began preparing herself later that afternoon and when she was nearly ready there came a knocking at the door. A girl who was with her went to open it but saw no one outside; it was neither dark nor light, for clouds alternately covered and uncovered the moon. The girl returned inside and said that she had seen no one, to which Guðrún replied, "This game is surely meant for me; I'll go." By that time she was dressed, save for her overcoat which she had yet to put on. She took it and put her arm through one sleeve, throwing the other over her shoulder and holding on to it with her hand.

When Guðrún stepped out of the house she saw Faxi standing near the door. A man whom she took to be the deacon stood next to him. Whether or not they spoke is not known; in any case he lifted Guðrún onto the horse and then mounted it himself in front of her. They set off and rode for a distance in silence, until they came to Hörgá river. Along it were high banks of ice and snow, and as the horse leapt over the edge the deacon's hat lifted at the back and Guðrún looked at his bare skull. At that moment the clouds parted and the apparition spoke, saying:

> The moon glides
> Death rides
> Don't you see the white spot
> At the nape of my neck,
> Garún, Garún?

Guðrún was stunned into silence and made no reply. Yet some say that Guðrún lifted the hat and, seeing the white skull, said, "I see what is." There are no reports of further exchanges between them, nor is anything known about the rest of their journey until they reached Myrká. They dismounted in front of the lichgate and the apparition spoke again, saying:

> Wait for me here, Garún, Garún,
> While I take Faxi, Faxi,
> To the edge of the yard, yard

It then led the horse away. Just then Guðrún looked into the churchyard and her eyes fell on an open grave. Terror gripped her, yet she had the wherewithal to grasp the bell-pull, and she began frantically ringing the church bells. Suddenly she felt someone seize her from behind. It was her good fortune that she had not put her overcoat on properly, for whatever seized her pulled so hard that the overcoat was torn in two along the sleeve that she was wearing. The last Guðrún saw of the apparition was that it fell headlong into the open grave still holding part of her cloak, while the earth swept down into it from both sides. Guðrún rang the bells incessantly until the residents at Myrká were roused and came out to fetch her; she was so rigid with fear that she could neither move from where she was nor stop ringing the bells. She was sure that she had been dealing with the deacon's ghost, even though she had been sent no word of his death. The Myrká residents confirmed this, telling her about the deacon's untimely death. She, in return, recounted her journey with his ghost.

That same night when the light had been turned out, the apparition returned to haunt Guðrún with such ferocity that all the Myrká residents were roused. No one slept a wink that night. For a fortnight afterwards Guðrún refused to be left alone and someone had to keep watch over her every night. Some say that the minister himself had to sit on the edge of her bed and read aloud from the Book of Psalms.

Finally a sorcerer from nearby Skagafjörður fjord was sent for. When he came he ordered that a boulder be unearthed from the ground above the hayfield and rolled over to the house gable. When darkness fell that evening the deacon's ghost once again appeared and tried to enter. The sorcerer forced it to move along the side of the house to the gable and then drove it into the ground with incantations, rolling the boulder over the top. It is said that the deacon's ghost remains there to this day.

Following this, all unearthly visitations ceased at Myrká, and Guðrún slowly recovered. She returned to Bægisá a short while later, but is reported to have never recovered fully from her ordeal.

Note: *In Icelandic, the name Guðrún means "divine mystery." Guð means "God." Legend has it that ghosts never utter God's name, nor any word containing "Guð." Thus the ghost is to have called Guðrún "Garún."*

The Vanished Bride

There once was a bachelor who lived on a small farm called Torfastaðakot, in Biskupstungur district, southwest Iceland. His name was Jón and he owned an abundance of sheep. When this story took place Jón was about to marry a young woman who was employed at his farm; it was in the autumn, just after the annual sheep round up. All necessary arrangements had been made, the date had been set and Jón had begun inviting guests to the wedding.

On the day that he set out to invite the last remaining guests, Jón accompanied his intended bride to a nearby brook where she planned to spend the day doing laundry. Jón then continued on his way, not returning until the late afternoon. As he passed the brook he noticed that some of the laundry remained unwashed beside it, some had been washed and some lay in the running water. He concluded that his intended must have felt ill and gone home. When he arrived back at the farm he asked about her, but was told that she had not returned and no one knew where she was. Jón grew worried. Together with a group of people he searched far and wide, but his bride was nowhere to be found. At length the search was called off and talk of the incident ceased, as did all speculation about the mysterious disappearance of Jón's bride.

Time passed, winter and summer came and went, and still there was no sign of the young woman. Then, one day, all of Jón's full-grown sheep disappeared at once. This was considered most strange. Jón searched the entire area near his farm but to no avail. He then enlisted the aid of another man to help him search further afield, and the two of them set off with provisions and a new pair of shoes. They looked everywhere, going on foot over mountains and across fields, until they were at the edge of Langjökull glacier. They decided to walk onto the glacier and continue on a distance northward in order to get a better view of the surrounding regions. But when they reached the top of the glacier they suddenly found themselves immersed in dense fog and a blinding snowstorm. They wandered aimlessly, without any idea where they were headed. After a time they perceived that they were on a downward slope. They picked up their pace and soon found themselves down in a valley, where there was no fog. It was late in the day. Off in the distance there was a farm, to which they made their way and knocked at the door. A woman opened. The two men asked whether they could possibly stay for the night; she replied that they could. They asked the name of the farm and where they were located, adding that they had been wandering about lost for most of the day. The woman then asked them where they thought they might be. They replied that they had to be somewhere in the northern parts, though they found it odd that they had come so far in such a short time. The woman then invited them in and told them that they would be informed of where they were in due course. She led the way through the main room and into an annex of the house, which was partitioned off from the rest. There she left them. As soon as she was gone another young woman came, holding a candle; she was about twenty years of age, vivacious and pretty. The two men ventured a greeting, to which the young woman replied amiably. She then proceeded to remove their wet outer clothing and did not stop until she had taken all their garments from them, right down to their socks and shoes. When they saw that she was going to leave with their clothing they grew anxious and asked her not to do so, for they were fearful for their own safety.

She replied that those were her orders and left with the garments, leaving the candle behind and locking the door. The two men remained inside and were very frightened.

Some time later they heard a knocking on the front door. Through a hole in the partition they watched as the woman who had initially received them went to the door holding a candle. She soon returned, and a man was with her. They stopped next to the door behind which the two men were kept, and the man began removing snow from his clothing.

"Did you find all the lambs?" the woman asked.

"Yes," replied the man.

"That is good," said the woman, and walked away.

A short while later came another knock at the door. Again the woman went to the door holding a candle; again she returned and a man was with her. They stopped in front of the door behind which the two men were kept, and the man began removing the snow from his clothing.

"Did you find all the rams?" the woman asked.

"Yes," replied the man.

"That is good," said the woman, and walked away.

A short while later came yet another knock at the door. As before, the woman went to the door holding a candle and soon returned, this time in the company of a man wearing a long cloak. She now began removing the snow from his clothing, in the same spot as the other two men had removed the snow from themselves. The cloaked man asked her whether anyone had come that day, to which she replied in the affirmative.

"Were all garments taken from the ruffians, including their socks and shoes?" he asked.

"Yes," she answered.

"Very good," he said. Then they left.

Upon hearing this the two men became even more frightened for they felt sure that the villains were plotting to kill them. However, a short while later the door to their quarters opened once more and the young woman who had taken their clothes came in with steaming bowls of fat mutton soup for them to eat. Having set those down she left again, locking the door behind her. Despite their fear, Jón and his companion devoured their food and, as they were utterly exhausted, soon fell asleep. They woke some time later to the sounds of the evening reading being performed in the main room. At this they were greatly relieved for they felt sure that the situation was not as threatening as they had initially feared, and they passed an uneventful night.

Early the next morning the young woman returned with clean and dry clothes, though not those that they had been wearing. She asked them to put them on, as they were to remain at the farm that day. She then left. Just when they had finished dressing she returned with some cold mutton for them, then left. While they were eating the woman who had first received them entered the room. She asked them from where they had come and they told her. She then asked for news from Biskupstungur district, which they provided to the best of their ability. The woman then asked whether they knew the farmer Jón in Torfastaðakot, if it was true that his bride had disappeared the previous year, how the area residents had reacted to the news, and how Jón was. They answered all her questions and then Jón told her who he was.

The woman then said that she was his vanished bride. "While I was doing the washing in the brook that day a man rode up on a horse. He seized me and brought me here. That man is the local county magistrate in these parts and he had recently lost his wife when he took me for his bride. He is not at home today, for he has been investigating a very serious and complex case of theft for the past two days. However, he wishes to speak with you," she said, turning to Jón, "and therefore he wants you to remain here for the day. He would like to make up to you the loss of your bride by offering you his daughter instead; she is the young woman who waited on you yesterday evening. He charmed your sheep here in order to meet with you, knowing that you would follow. They shall be returned to you when you leave this place." Jón and his companion were delighted to hear this. They remained at the farm for the day, were attended to in every way and enjoyed themselves the best they could.

That evening the county magistrate returned home, but did not meet with his guests until the following morning. It is not known how long Jón and the magistrate spoke, but the outcome of their meeting was just as the woman had said. The magistrate told Jón to come back the following spring for his daughter and either have the same man with him or come alone. Furthermore, he should bring with him as many pack horses as he wanted and the magistrate would load them up with goods; he considered this a better prospect than giving Jón sheep, for sheep would surely run away from their new surroundings during the course of the summer. When they left the magistrate returned all of Jón's sheep and accompanied the two men as far as necessary.

The following spring Jón returned to the farm as arranged, taking the same man with him, along with twelve saddled horses. The magistrate gave Jón his daughter's hand in marriage and then loaded up the horses with food and provisions of every sort. Upon returning to Torfastaðakot Jón married the magistrate's daughter. Their union was a happy one; both of them lived to a ripe old age and they had a great number of descendants.

It is thought that the outlaw settlement told of in this tale was in either Hvinverjadalir or Þjófadalir valleys, at the northern end of Langjökull glacier. And thus ends this story.

Note: *"Provisions and a new pair of shoes"* – nesti og nýja skó *in the original – is a very common phrase in Icelandic folk tales. People hardly ever set off on long journeys without something to eat and a new pair of shoes. This is probably because the shoes back then were made of sheep leather with no hard soles, and they wore out very quickly. So it was absolutely essential to have a spare pair of shoes in the very likely event that the previous pair would fall apart halfway through your journey.*

The Legend
of Úlfsvatn Lake

At the bottom of Skagafjörður fjord in the north of Iceland there are several valleys leading inland. Between them and the sea lies a fishing lake known as Úlfsvatn. This is the legend of how the lake got its name.

There once lived a wealthy farmer at a farm called Mælifellsá. He had a son named Guðmundur, a fine young man in every respect who was both physically strong and a good wrestler. Guðmundur frequently took part in the annual roundup of sheep down from the highlands in the autumn, often leading his team of herders.

After the initial gathering of the sheep it was customary to go out and search the area once more, to ensure that no sheep had been left behind. On one such occasion Guðmundur went out along with several other men. They divided into groups and Guðmundur teamed up with a young boy. The two of them walked until they reached Úlfsvatn lake; there they found two stray lambs that they began chasing. The lake was frozen over and out on it was a man, fishing through a hole in the ice. As Guð- mundur and the boy drew closer the man suddenly got to his feet and picked up an axe that lay next to him, sliding across the ice to where Guðmundur and the boy were standing. When the boy saw the strang- er approach he bolted off, but Guðmundur stood his ground. When the outlaw was close enough he brought the axe down on Guðmundur, who man- aged to dodge it at the last moment. The outlaw then accidentally dropped the axe; Guðmundur seized it and slid out onto the ice, with the outlaw close be- hind. A chase ensued, until Guðmundur saw an op- portunity to spin around and deal the outlaw a fatal blow with the axe. As the axe struck him, the outlaw shouted for Brandur, Þorgils and Ólafur.

Guðmundur hurried back and told the other men what had happened. They returned to the lake in large numbers, only to find that the dead man's body had been taken away. A trail of blood led away from the lake.

After this incident, Guðmundur stayed close to home and stopped taking part in the round up, for it was feared that the outlaws might lie in wait for him. Late one summer, however, the shepherd at Mælifellsá became ill and no one was there to herd the sheep home but Guðmundur. He set off but could not find the sheep anywhere. He walked onto the nearby moors but they were nowhere to be seen. While Guðmundur searched there, a dense fog set in so that he lost his way. After wandering blindly for a time he chanced upon a large herd of sheep with a man standing nearby. As soon as the outlaw saw Guðmundur he rushed at him; they wrestled long and hard, until Guðmundur had the better of him. The outlaw then pleaded with Guðmundur to spare his life, swearing that he would be generously rewarded if he did.

Guðmundur asked the man his name and where he lived. The outlaw replied that his name was Óla-fur, "And the man killed on the lake was my brother Úlfur. There are now six of us brothers and I am the youngest and smallest. My father lives on a farm not far away and he has lured you here to avenge himself on you for killing his son; he has dug a grave in the farmyard, which he intends to be your resting place. We also have a sister named Sigríður; our fa-ther loves her the best and she could do most to help you, provided she wants to. My brother Brandur is not far from here and if you were to fell him as you felled me, thereby sparing both our lives, she would be sure to aid you in any way she could."

Guðmundur released Ólafur and then went on until he found Brandur. They wrestled, and

Guðmundur felled him like he had his brother. Brandur then pleaded with Guðmundur to spare his life and swore his allegiance, as Ólafur had done. Guðmundur released him and walked on until he reached the farm. He came upon Sigríður outside and conveyed regards from her brothers, along with their wishes that she help him, for he had spared their lives.

Sigríður led Guðmundur to a loft above the cowshed and fetched wine for him to drink, which greatly revived him. She told him about the open pit in the farmyard and advised him to retreat from her father to the edge of it, and then to leap across it at the last moment. Her father would fall headlong in; however, Guðmundur must not kill him.

Her father was now sleeping, she said, but would soon awaken and know of Guðmundur's arrival; he should go to the front of the house and knock on the door. Guðmundur did as she said. When the old man heard the knocking he rose from his bed, remarking that Guðmundur had arrived and that his reputed manliness would now be put to the test. He then rushed out and charged at Guðmundur without further ado. A savage struggle ensued. Guðmundur soon realized that the old man was twice as strong as he; thus he concentrated on defending himself and refrained from assault. The old man drove him backwards to the grave and Guðmundur went along, leaping across the pit at the last moment so that the old man fell in headlong.

Just then Sigríður arrived with the two brothers that Guðmundur had wrestled with. They pleaded with him to spare their father's life and Guðmundur agreed to this, provided they would not harm him from then on. The old man gave Guðmundur his solemn vow that they would not and was subsequently pulled up from the grave. He thanked Guðmundur for sparing his life and invited him to enter the house, yet he also remarked that he could not be sure of how his elder sons would take to Guðmundur's presence when they arrived home. Guðmundur was then given something to eat and drink and later that evening was shown to his lodgings and locked inside. When the elder sons returned home they asked whether Guðmundur was now resting in the grave. Their father told them what had happened, to which they reacted with furious anger, threatening to break down the door to Guðmundur's room. The old man blocked the way, saying that they would have to get past him first if they insisted on violating Guðmundur's sanctuary. At this they calmed down somewhat and at length went to bed. In the morning their father let them in to see Guðmundur but forbade them from laying a hand on him.

Guðmundur remained weather-bound at the farm for the entire winter. During that time he and

Sigríður formed an attachment; she was a handsome woman and so strong that she was quite her brothers' equal.

When spring came Guðmundur longed to return to Skagafjörður and Sigríður, who by this time was with child, desired to go with him. Her father made no objection and she accompanied Guðmundur back home. They journeyed nonstop until they reached Mælifellsá, where Guðmundur was received with such jubilation that it was as though he had been raised from the dead. Guðmundur lived at Mælifellsá for many years and married Sigríður, who was considered a fine woman. One by one her brothers also moved to the settled area, as their lives had become lonely and dull after her departure and the death of their father. Some of them became farmers in Skagafjörður and were considered men of great vigor and strength.

The Hidden Man
and the Girl

There once was an adolescent girl who lived with her mother. The mother was a widow who had managed her own farm since the death of her husband. The girl's task was to watch over the livestock.

Early one morning she went past a knoll. A man stood next to it; he appeared very distressed and asked the girl to come into the knoll and assist his wife, for she was in the throes of childbirth and in dire need of help. He said that his name was Arnljótur. The girl, however, refused to go with him. Later that day she told her mother of the incident. Her mother reproached her for not having been more helpful and sternly advised her to grant the hidden man his request if he were to approach her again. The next morning the man once again approached the girl with the same request, but she refused. On the third morning he appeared again and said that his wife was now about to die. The girl relented and went inside the knoll. The hidden man's wife bore three children before she died. The girl bathed the children and swaddled them, laid them all in one bed, said a prayer and made the sign of the cross over them. But as she was about to turn from the bed she stumbled, fell on one of the children, and crushed it to death. Arnljótur followed her outside and told her that it must now be obvious to her that she should have complied with his request right away. He added that although she had been careless with the child, he did not hold her responsible, for it had been an accident. He then gave her three objects in parting and asked her to give his regards to her mother and to thank her for the good advice she had given. For when the girl had twice refused to help Arnljótur her mother had said that she had better grant his request on the third occasion, otherwise she did not want to see the girl again.

Some time later, Arnljótur approached the girl once more and asked her to go to the knoll with him and marry him, otherwise the children would perish in his hands. He entreated her to do this for him but once again she absolutely refused. Some time passed and one day a man arrived at the farm. When he saw the objects that the hidden man had given the girl he asked to have them and offered other, even more splendid ones in exchange. The girl rejected his offer outright, saying that under no circumstances would she part with the objects that her Arnljótur had given her.

The next day Arnljótur appeared where the girl sat, separating brushwood. "You did well not to part with the objects that I gave you and have proven your loyalty to me," he said. "Now do as I bid you; come with me and live with me, you shall want for nothing and no harm shall ever befall you." However, as before, the girl flatly refused. Then the man said, "You are stubborn; others will also find you so and it shall prove a burden to you. Your life shall never be prosperous, yet those women whom you assist in childbirth shall always be safe and in that way you shall earn your living." He then vanished. When the girl returned home she found that both her mother and the objects had disappeared; Arnljótur had taken them with him. And Arnljótur's words came to pass: the girl did not have a prosperous life, was restless and nomadic, yet was considered an exceptional midwife.

Kráka the Ogre

In former times there lived an ogre known as Kráka in a cave at Bláhvammur hollow, in Bláfjall mountain. Remnants of this cave are still visible. The rock face leading up to it is very steep and virtually impossible for mortal beings to climb. Kráka was a menacing creature who preyed on the area farmers' sheep and caused numerous deaths, both of animals and people. She had taken a liking to the masculine sex and had an aversion to being alone, thus she frequently abducted men from the inhabited regions and kept them in her cave. The majority of them could by no means resign themselves to their fate, however; most either ran away or took their own lives.

On one occasion Kráka abducted a shepherd named Jón who lived at the farm Baldursheimur. She kept him in her cave and offered him the best food and drink, but he would have none of her hospitality. She tried her best to make him eat, but to no avail. Finally the shepherd said that he would only regain his appetite if he were given twelve-year-old cured shark to eat. Kráka, through her powers of witchcraft, knew that the only place to obtain twelve-year-old cured shark was in Siglunes, in the north. And though that was a mighty long way off, she decided that it would be worth her while to see if she could get the shark.

She set off, leaving the shepherd behind in her cave. When she had gone a fair distance it suddenly occurred to her that the shepherd might have tricked her and run away as soon as she was out of sight, and that it might be best to go back and check. She ran as fast as her legs would carry her, only to find that the shepherd was still in the cave. She set off again, but when she had gone slightly further than before she began to have the same nagging doubt that the shepherd might have betrayed her. Again she rushed back to the cave as fast as she could but, as before, she found the shepherd still there. A third time she set off, utterly convinced this time that the shepherd would not be up to any tricks. She took the shortest route to Siglunes, crossing Eyjafjörður fjord to the north of Hrísey island. Her journey was uneventful; she obtained the shark and set off home by the same route.

Meanwhile, the shepherd waited until he estimated Kráka to be at her destination, then got to his feet and ran off in the direction of home. Shortly afterwards Kráka arrived at the cave to find him gone. She turned on her heels and rushed after him. As the shepherd was approaching Baldursheimur farm he became aware of rumblings in the ground behind him and guessed that it was Kráka. When she was within shouting distance of him, she called out, "Here is the shark, Jón, cured not 12 but 13 years," to which he made no reply. When the shepherd at last reached the farm he found the yeoman working iron in his forge, and he ran in past him, just as Kráka appeared in the doorway. The yeoman took the red-hot iron from the furnace and rushed at Kráka, threatening to drive it into her unless she turned around that very instant and never ventured to disturb him or his people again. Kráka saw that she had no choice but to turn back and she is not known to have bothered the Baldursheimur farmer after that.

On another occasion Kráka abducted a shepherd from the farm Grænavatn and took him to her cave; as with his predecessor this one refused anything that Kráka offered him, much to her disappointment. In the end the shepherd told her that the only thing he could possibly eat was the fresh meat of a male goat. At that time goats were kept on only one farm in Iceland, Hafrafellstunga in Axarfjörður. And although that was a long distance from Bláhvammur hollow, Kráka decided she would try and obtain what the shepherd wanted. Before she left, however, she took a huge boulder and placed it at the mouth of the cave, for under no circumstance did she want to lose this shepherd like the last one. She took the shortest route to her destination and when she came to the glacial river Jökulsá á fjöllum she leapt over it, from one cliff to another. Today that place is still known as Skessuhlaup, which may be translated as Ogre Sprint.

The rest of the journey was uneventful. When Kráka reached Hafrafellstunga farm she caught two bucks, tied them together by the horns and threw them across her shoulder. She then headed back the same way she had come, crossing Jökulsá á fjöllum in the same place as before. When she had leapt across the river the second time she found that she was weary from her trip and decided to rest. She untied the bucks and set them out to graze in a ravine that since has been known as Hafragil, or Buck Ravine. When Kráka had rested a while she tied the bucks together once more and continued on her way.

Meanwhile, after Kráka left, the shepherd tried all he could to escape from the cave, but found neither a crack in the cave wall through which he could flee, nor a space to hide. At length he stumbled on a large, sharp sword belonging to Kráka. With it he was able to carve an opening into the boulder blocking the cave opening, large enough for him to slip through. He made his way back to the inhabited area as quickly as he could and is presumed to have arrived there safe and sound.

Another time Kráka was planning a large Christmas celebration, for which she took great pains to prepare. The only thing that was missing, in her opinion, was a bit of human flesh, which she considered the greatest delicacy. Thus on Christmas Eve she set off for the inhabited region to see what she might find. But when she came to the uppermost farms in Mývatnssveit district she discovered that they were all empty of people, for everyone had gone to attend mass at Skútustaðir. As Kráka was not satisfied to go back empty-handed she carried on until she reached Skútustaðir. By then everyone was already inside the church. Kráka went to the church door and spotted a man sitting on a corner pew near the door. She reached for him, hoping to snatch him from the church, but he fiercely resisted and shouted at the top of his lungs for help, which came instantly. In the end the entire congregation was working to free the man from Kráka's grasp, but she held on so long that one of the church walls cracked. At this Kráka reportedly became very angry and declared that the church wall should never be steady again.

This is thought to have had all the power of a curse, for the southern wall of Skútustaðir church has been rickety ever since.

People also say that Kráka swore to wreak all the destruction that she could on the people of upper Mývatnssveit district, more than they would ever forget. At that time there was a large lake on one of the district's summer pastures. Kráka went there and uprooted a large number of trees and shrubs, which she placed in a heap. Next she loaded rocks and turf on top, so that the heap was both broad and heavy. Then she dragged this massive load away from the lake, down into Mývatnssveit and the length of the district to where the Laxá river flows out of Lake Mývatn. It made a deep and wide indentation in the countryside into which Kráka directed water from the lake, while at the same time she pronounced that, from then on, the river should ravage the pastures and other land belonging to the people of Mývatnssveit. The only materials that might stem the tide of destruction would be the same as were used in her load, though the river would nevertheless wreak havoc in the upper part of the district.

Today that river still flows along the same indentation. It is known as Krákuá river and it has proven to be the bane of the people of Mývatnssveit district. It flows the length of the Mývatnssveit pastures and each spring tears large chunks out of its own banks, depositing sand and clay onto the pastures. As a result, parts of Mývatnssveit district are being turned into a wasteland, even though each year the holes are filled with shrubs, rocks and turf – the same materials Kráka is said to have used in her load. Thus some old and wise people suspect that Kráka's proclamations and curses are coming to pass.

Þorgeir's Bull

There once was a man named Þorgeir whom many called Geir the Sorcerer. He had a brother named Stefán, sometimes called Stefán the Chanter, for it was said that he chanted and sang exceptionally well. Their surname was Jónsson. There was also a third man whose name was Andrés; he was their maternal uncle. All three came from Fnjóskadalur valley in the north of the country and sailed out to fish from Hrísey island in Eyjafjörður fjord. These men are all reported to have taken part in creating the bull.

Þorgeir is said to have obtained a newborn calf from a woman on Hrísey. He slit its hide where he thought best and skinned it as far back as the loins – some say even further back than the loins – so that the calf dragged its hide on its tail. He then endowed the beast with magical powers. Still, the three men were not satisfied and so they set into the wound the characteristics of eight different entities: air, bird, man, dog, cat, mouse and two different sea monsters. Thus the bull had nine natures, including its own. It could travel through air just as easily as through sea and across land, and it could appear in the guises of all nine entities at will. Despite all this Þorgeir could still not be sure of the bull's invulnerability, so he obtained a baby's caul to cover it with. And as it was primarily Þorgeir who had created the bull and endowed it with magical powers, the beast became known as Þorgeir's Bull. Besides, it was mostly Þorgeir who used the bull to carry out various misdeeds.

As it happened, Þorgeir had proposed to a woman named Guðrún Bessadóttir, but she had refused him. Thus the three men sent the bull after her. It took some time for the beast to begin disrupting Guðrún's life, but before too long she was scarcely able to turn around without being harassed. When she went from one farm to another she often had to be escorted by six to eight men, for not many felt safe around her. Sometimes she would be torn from her horse and flung three or four yards despite being accompanied by so many men; at other times she was completely left in peace. In the end she was killed as a result of injuries inflicted upon her by the bull.

On one occasion Guðrún was in church when the bull took to tormenting her so aggressively that she developed intense convulsions and nearly injured herself. A man who left the church said that when he came out he saw the bull lying on the side of a nearby house. One side of the house faced the church, the other away from it, and the bull lay on that side.

It had its nose resting on the ridge of the roof so that the man could see into its open nostrils. To him it seemed as if there were a grey current running from the nostrils to the church. When he went around to the side of the house on which the bull lay, he saw it disappear.

There was a farmer at Sund in Höfðahverfi district whose name was Magnús. His wife Helga was a close relative of Guðrún Bessadóttir. After Guðrún's death the bull took to tormenting Helga. A sorcerer named Torfi who lived at Klúkur in Eyjafjörður fjord was sent for. He was asked to slay the bull, to deliver Helga from her predicament. When Torfi came to Sund he could see the bull lying above Helga in the main room. She was distressed about the weight that was on her, particularly on her naked feet, on which the bull seemed to be lying. Torfi could not slay the bull because, according to him, he did not know whether the baby's caul had been removed from the head down or the feet up; the method for removing it varied. In any case the bull would be difficult to overpower while the caul was still on. In the end the bull is said to have caused Helga's death and to have hounded her relatives for a long time after that.

Although Þorgeir originally planned to use the bull only to kill Guðrún, he continued to have it harass those on whom he wanted to avenge himself. The beast was exceedingly loyal to Þorgeir, who often sent it out to ride and pester other men's cows so that they were frequently led astray. Also, the bull could often be heard howling in darkness and fog. Once, Þorgeir was a guest at a farm called Hallgilsstaðir during the evening reading. He had a tendency to leave the premises while the evening readings were taking place, for they were usually from the Scriptures. After that particular reading the yeoman walked outside with Þorgeir. Off in the distance they noticed something resembling a strip of fog, though the sky was otherwise clear. Þorgeir then remarked, "Damn, it sure has stretched itself out." Those who were with him took Þorgeir to mean the bull and assumed that it was appearing in one of its guises, that of fog. A short while later there was a fierce blizzard and the farm people whispered that the bull must have known that it was coming. Indeed, after that such a phenomenon was said to frequently precede bad weather or other remarkable incidents. There were also reports from the north of Iceland that two infamous ghosts, Húsavíkur-Lalli and Eyjafjarðar-Skotta, teamed up with Þorgeir's Bull, travelling the length of the Fnjóská river while sitting on the bull's hide, which it dragged along behind it.

When the bull started having trouble carrying out Þorgeir's orders, it returned home and turned on its master, playing various pranks on him and even threatening to kill him. And although Þorgeir certainly knew a thing or two about sorcery, he was often at a loss when it came to defending himself against the bull's assaults. If the beast was feeling particularly aggressive he was forced to double his efforts. Once the bull tried so hard to kill Þorgeir that he fled helplessly into the farmhouse where his wife sat with their infant child in her arms. Þorgeir, in his desperation, wanted to take the child to give to the bull, hoping thus to pacify the beast. His wife begged him not to, telling him instead to take a newborn calf from the barn to give to the bull. Þorgeir assented, loosened the calf and sent it out of the barn. Some time later it was found dead nearby, torn into tiny pieces.

There are no reports of the bull committing ill deeds after that; at worst it is said to have driven cows mad. However, it preyed upon Þorgeir's relatives and Þorgeir insisted that his daughters, who were both named Ingibjörg, carry magic runes in their aprons for protection. When the bull appeared it did so in various guises, sometimes in the form of a man or a dog, but most often in the likeness of a bull with horns, skinned back to its tail and dragging its bloody hide behind it. Regardless of its guise the beast was considered utterly hideous in appearance and most people were terrified of it. It is also said that the bull outlived Þorgeir, for he had not managed to slay it before he died. Some say that, when he lay on his deathbed, a grey cat – some say a black pup – lay curled up on his chest, and that this would have been one of the bull's guises. Some people claim that the bull was created at the beginning of the eighteenth century; others say that it was near the middle of that century.

Note: *If you find yourself completely baffled by this story, don't worry – you are in good company. As I mentioned in the introduction, my first thought when I read this was: What were those people on? (I mean, seriously: two daughters – and both named Ingibjörg?) The more times I read it, the more I find it likely that these folks had partaken of that rotten flour my husband mentioned, or some other hallucinatory substance. Incidentally, a kind reader has put up a very interesting analysis of the story on this book's amazon.com page, in case anyone is interested.*

The Outlaw on Kiðuvallafjall Mountain

Once in bygone days a man and his wife lived at the far end of a valley in the east of the country. Their names are not known, but they had a young daughter named Helga who was both fair and wholesome in appearance. The couple kept a hired hand named Jón, a loyal, hard-working young man with a keen mind who was well liked by all who knew him. Jón and Helga formed an attachment and fell in love. When Helga's parents learned of their mutual affection they opposed it, claiming that Jón was not a suitable husband for their daughter and, moreover, had neither security nor property. Yet under no circumstances did they want to lose him, for they prized his diligent and loyal nature. Thus they treated him well. Jón did not relinquish his position, for to do so would mean leaving Helga behind, and so he remained at the farm for many years. They continued to love one another, albeit chastely, and waited for an opportunity to be united.

At the furthest edge of the farm property was a valley named Kiðuvalladalur, after the Kiðuvellir plains that lay at one end. A great mountain named Kiðuvallafjall rose there. This was bounteous land where in spring and autumn livestock was put out to pasture. It was also very remote. One day when Jón was herding livestock down the mountain he heard a loud voice calling from somewhere further down, "Kiðuvalla, Kiðuvalla, alone I live on a mountain!" Jón was greatly perplexed, for he could see no one and there were no hiding places in the area. He concluded that he must have been mistaken and drove the livestock home.

The following day he was once again herding livestock on the mountain when he heard the call again in the same place, even more clearly than before: "Kiðuvalla, Kiðuvalla, alone I live on a mountain!" Jón thought the voice came from a large boulder and ran there but saw nothing. He sat down and all at once was seized with a curious intoxication and drowsiness, so that he fell asleep. It then seemed to Jón as though a kindly stranger appeared before him, greeting him amiably. Jón returned the greeting and asked who the man was. "I am an outlaw," the apparition answered, "and I live inside this large boulder. I am the one you have twice heard calling. I did it to draw you to this place but I could not meet you, for I am on my deathbed. Today the boulder is not open but tomorrow when you come to do the herding it shall be. Meet me then." It seemed to Jón that he agreed to this. He then woke and drove the livestock home. Once there he told Helga all about the boulder dweller. She replied that the man was surely in dire need and entreated Jón not to let him down. Jón promised to do all he could.

When he arrived at the boulder again it was open. Jón went in and found an ailing man lying on a bed of sheepskin. This was the same man who had appeared before him. He greeted Jón warmly and said, "You have done well to come. Soon my twelve-year stay here shall be over. I was sentenced to death for committing incest and fled here. I knew stone masonry; I took tools with me and carved out this stone, as well as other smaller ones in the area for storage. This one here has proven himself a most loyal ally," he added, pointing to a large, black dog that lay at his feet with its gaze fixed on its master. "This I ask of you, that you keep me company in my remaining hours," said the outlaw.

"Then I will run home and inform of my absence," answered Jón. The outlaw agreed.

Jón ran home and asked for leave to take a long journey. He was granted his request. When he returned to the boulder its occupant was still alive. He told Jón, "All my earthly belongings I bequeath to you, including this chest of money at my feet and the black dog, who shall prove a most valuable and devoted friend. I also ask that you bury me here, next to the boulder."

Jón promised to do so, and thanked the outlaw for the gifts. He then remained with him until he died. Jón prepared the body for burial and buried it next to the boulder as the outlaw had requested. After securing the black dog's affections he returned home and related all to Helga. He told her that they were now exceedingly wealthy, adding, "And let us now move to the boulder." They ran off secretly to the boulder and remained there until Helga's parents died; after that they returned to the farm and lived there until they were both very old. Thus ends this story.

In Brúaröræfi, in the Icelandic outback, is a valley named Kiðuvalladalur with a mountain rising high above it. That might be the location described in this tale.

The Hidden Woman's Curse

I n the middle of the last century there lived a man named Jón Árnason; he was a bachelor and resided with his mother and father in Bárðardalur valley, north Iceland. Jón is reputed to have been a keenly observant and trustworthy man.

Once Jón went to transport sulphur along with several other men from the sulphur mines south of Lake Mývatn, in the north. The nearest resting place to the mines was Heilagsdalur valley and those travelling back from the mines usually took a break from their journey there.

Nothing of consequence is known to have happened to the men on their journey back from the mines, that is until they reached Heilagsdalur valley.

There they unsaddled their horses and set up camp for the night.

That same night Jón dreamt that a woman of strong build and dressed in blue appeared before him. She asked Jón to rise and accompany her, which he did. They walked for a distance, until Jón began to have grave doubts about what he was doing and decided that it would be safer to return to the camp. The woman pleaded with him to go with her and assured him that no harm would befall him; on the contrary, he would have much good fortune if he did. Yet Jón remained adamant and they parted ways.

In the morning Jón's companions woke to find him missing and began searching for him. After a time they saw him running towards them. They asked him where he had been but Jón gave no answer. The group then decamped and set off for home.

Two or three nights after arriving there, Jón dreamed that the same woman appeared before him as when he slept in Heilagsdalur valley. She was furiously angry and said something to this effect: "You did an ill deed, Jón, by not coming with me when I asked you the last time. I want you to know that my request was without guile and sprang from a most dire need. My daughter was in the throes of giving birth and could only do so with the assistance of a mortal being. Had you delivered me and her from that awful predicament you would indeed have become a man of great fortune; instead she has died a horrible death. From now on your life shall be filled with adversity and misfortune, though even that is not punishment enough for you. I cannot rest without giving you scars to remember me by."

She then walked over to Jón, put one hand to his throat and tightened her grip like a vice, so that he woke with a start. As he opened his eyes, he saw the woman vanish.

Jón soon experienced such intense pain and swelling of the throat that it was close to unbearable. Nothing could alleviate his suffering; rather it increased in severity until those around him began to fear that this strange and sudden affliction would end his life. What the cause of it was he told no one.

On the third night of his illness Jón dreamed that another woman dressed in blue appeared before him, this one somewhat more kindly. She said: "My sister does you an injustice, for you could not have known her intent when she asked you to accompany her; thus you suffer unfairly. I want to help you, as best I can. Tomorrow, if you are well enough, take your horse and ride to Krosshlíð slope, to the north of Ljósavatnsskarð mountain pass. An abundance of herbs and grasses grow there. When you are about halfway up you will come to a brook; follow it until you have reached the center of the slope. There, in a grassy hollow, grow some herbs that you must take and lay on your throat. You shall find them by my direction."

Having thus spoken, the woman disappeared. When Jón woke up he felt worse than ever; yet he managed to mount his horse and ride to Krosshlíð slope. There he found the herbs, as the woman in blue had instructed, and as soon as he laid them on his throat his pain disappeared. Within a few days Jón had recovered completely and he lived on to become an old man. It is said, however, that he came up against a great deal of adversity in his life and that he did not tell anyone the story of the hidden women until much later in his life.

Satan Takes
a Wife

There once were a mother and daughter who
lived together. They were women of substantial wealth and the younger one was considered an
excellent prospect for marriage. She had a number
of suitors, none of which she accepted. Consequently people began to believe that she intended to live
a chaste life and to serve God, for she was extremely
God-fearing. This was something that Satan could
not tolerate. He disguised himself as a young man,
courted the girl, and eventually proposed marriage.
His intention, of course, was to gradually win power
over her. Satan managed to make himself appear so
honest and sincere that the girl accepted his proposal,

the contract was drawn up and they were married. But on their wedding night, when he was about to lie down with her, he found her so pure and untainted that he could not bear to be near her. He came up with the excuse that he must have a bath prepared for him if he were to get any rest at all. Thus a bath was prepared, in which Satan proceeded to sit the entire night.

The following day he wandered outside, thinking only of how to extract himself from this hapless situation. By chance he met a man walking down the road, with whom he made a deal to replace him as the girl's husband. He then cast the guise he had assumed over the man. In exchange, the man promised to let Satan have his oldest child when it reached the age of seven; he would bring the child to the place where they were now standing and leave it there. The man then went to the girl, who assumed him to be her husband and received him happily. Their relationship flourished and she bore one son, whom they both loved very much.

Time passed, and when the boy was six years old his father took to brooding for long periods of time. His wife pressed him as to the reason for his melancholy and eventually he told her the entire story. Her response was that she had indeed been too long deceived; nonetheless she proposed a solution.

On the boy's seventh birthday, his father took him to the place where he and Satan had last parted, drew a circle around it and consecrated the place with holy song. He then remained with his son until the evening. Before leaving he told him that, no matter what he would see that night, he must not step out of the circle unless it was at the bidding of someone who extended a hand into it in Jesus' name. When the boy's father had gone, various friends and acquaintances began to appear who tried to entice him out of the circle with delicacies and sweets. Next, his parents appeared and alternately asked kindly or demanded angrily that the boy come to them. After that he saw a number of children playing with toys of every description, who called out for him to join them. But the boy stood his ground, for no one had extended a hand into the circle in Jesus' name. Finally flying sparks, voracious flames, grotesque images and fantastic visions appeared, continuing until morning. Still the boy did not leave the circle, despite being frightened out of his wits. At the first break of dawn his parents came to fetch him, extending their hands into the circle. And thus Satan was deprived of his end of the bargain.

The Church Builder

There once lived a man at the farm Reynir, in Mýrdalur valley, south Iceland. He was to raise a church there, but lacked wood for its construction. The haymaking season was upon him and there were no carpenters to help him with the building, thus he began to fear that the church would not be constructed before the onset of winter.

One day he was wandering about in his fields with a heavy heart when a man approached and offered to build the church for him. In exchange the farmer was to guess his name before the construction was completed; if the farmer failed to do so then he was to give the man his only son, who at that time was five years old. The farmer agreed to this.

The stranger then began working, focusing on few things outside of his work and speaking very little. As a result the construction of the church moved along quickly and the farmer gradually realized that if this pace were to continue it would be fully built by the end of the haymaking season. At this he became increasingly despondent but felt that he could in no way alter the course of events.

One day in autumn, when construction of the church was nearly completed, the farmer wandered out beyond the edge of his hayfield. He came to a knoll and lay down. Suddenly, from within the knoll, he heard chanting, as though a mother were singing to her child. This is what he heard:

> Finnur, your father, will not make you wait
> Much longer for your little playmate.

This was sung over and over again. The farmer was greatly relieved when he heard this; he walked homewards directly and went straight to the church. Inside, the stranger had just finished fitting the last board for the altar and was about to fasten it. The farmer said, "It looks as though you shall soon be finished, Finnur, my friend." When the stranger heard this he received such a jolt that he dropped the board and vanished. He has not been seen since.

Hagridden

here once was a parson who was both wealthy and kind. He was newly married when this story took place, to a young and beautiful woman whom he loved very much. She was considered one of the most exceptional women in the region at that time. Yet there was one flaw in her behavior that upset the parson greatly: every Christmas Eve she would disappear without informing anyone where she went. The parson entreated her to tell him, but she always replied that it was none of his business. This was the only thing that cast a shadow on their otherwise harmonious marriage.

Once, the parson happened to take in a young drifter. The youth was small and feeble-minded, yet it was whispered that he knew a great deal more than most people. Time passed and Christmas approached. On Christmas Eve the youth was in the stable, tending the parson's horses. Suddenly the parson's wife came in and began conversing with him on a variety of subjects. Then, without warning, she took a bridle from beneath her apron and put it on him. This bridle was endowed with such magical powers that the youth passively allowed the parson's wife to mount him, after which he bolted out of the stable and off, like a bird taking flight. He flew across mountains and valleys, rocks and cliffs, crossing anything they encountered along the way.

After some time they arrived at a small house. The parson's wife dismounted and tied the youth to a peg that was sticking out of the side of the house. Then she went around the front and knocked at the door. A man answered and greeted her with delight before leading her inside. As soon as they had gone in the youth freed himself and also managed to remove the bridle, which he kept with him. He then crept onto the roof of the house and through an opening was able to observe what was happening inside. He saw twelve women sitting around a table; the man who had come to the door was number thirteen. The youth recognized the parson's wife among them. These women bore the utmost respect for the man. They were recounting to him various tales of their trickery and cunning and the parson's wife boasted that she had come riding on the back of a living man. The master of the house clearly considered this a tremendous feat and declared reverently that riding a living man was a hag ride of the highest order. He added that her powers of witchcraft must be exceptional, "For I have never known anyone to achieve that, except myself." The rest of the women grew very excited and entreated him to teach them this particular craft. The man then placed a book on the table; it had grey pages and was written in glowing embers, or with letters that were the color of glowing embers. The letters radiated light throughout the entire house, this being the only source of light there was. The master of the house then began teaching the women how to use the book, explaining to them the nature of its contents. Meanwhile the youth outside listened carefully, hanging onto every word.

Morning approached and the women began saying that it would soon be time to leave; thus the lesson was brought to an end. Then each woman took out a glass, which they handed to the master of the house. The youth could see that the glasses contained a red liquid, and that the man drank this liquid before handing the glasses back to the women. Each then cordially took their leave of him and left the house. The youth noticed that each of the women had her own bridle and each rode some object: one had the leg bone of a horse, another a jaw, a third a shoulder blade, and so on. They mounted their steeds and rode off. The parson's wife, however, could not find her mount anywhere. In a mad fury she raged around the house and just when she was least expecting it the youth hopped down from the roof and immediately bridled her. He then mounted her and set off for home. He had learned enough that night to steer the parson's wife in the right direction, and they journeyed without incident until they were back in the stable from which they had departed. There the youth dismounted, fastening the parson's wife so that she remained inside the stable. He then went into the house and recounted his journey to the farm people, telling them where he had been, what he had seen and where the parson's wife was now. Naturally all were very shaken, particularly the parson. Then the parson's wife was brought in and the truth was demanded from her. In the end she confessed that she and eleven other parsons' wives had been enrolled in the so-called Black School, that Lucifer himself had been instructing them in witchcraft, and that a mere one year remained of their study. She also said that Lucifer had demanded to be given their menstrual blood as payment; this had been the red liquid that the youth had seen in the glasses. Having thus confessed, the parson's wife was duly punished for her wicked ways.

Fostered by
a Hidden Woman

There once was a small child, scarcely two years of age, that had just learned to speak. One day this child believed it saw its mother walk behind a knoll in the hay field. It followed her until the knoll had blocked the farmhouse from view; then the woman walked into the knoll and the child followed. The child, who was a girl, was brought up by the hidden woman until she was thirteen. The hidden woman, who was elderly, was very kind to the girl and taught her many things, both intellectual and practical. She learned all the Psalms and songs that were commonly known in Iceland at the time, and she also learned others, which had a spiritual quality but which nevertheless seemed foreign and strange. The girl never saw anyone other than her foster mother and she was very content, though she had a hazy remembrance of having lived somewhere else at one time.

Eventually the hidden woman contracted an illness that led to her death. Before she died she thanked the girl for her loyalty and devotion and said that it would now be best for her to return to her parents' care. She told her that they would remember her and that she would marry, be prosperous and well liked by all who knew her. The hidden woman then gave the girl various objects to remember her by, including a headdress with a veil. She also told the girl that, when the time came that something happened to the headdress, it would be a sign that she would not have much time left to live. They then bid each other a fond farewell.

The girl became a woman of extraordinary good fortune. She married a kind and wealthy man, their marriage lasted many years and they had a number of children, all of whom became well educated. One autumn day, when she was an old woman, she went to church with her husband to take the sacrament. She wore the headdress that the hidden woman had given her. That evening, after returning from church, she removed the headdress and was preparing to lock it away when she noticed that the veil was torn. She then called her husband and children to her and told them this story, offered them her wisdom and advice, and then retired. She fell asleep and never woke up again.

Búkolla

There once were an old man and woman who owned a small farm. They had one son, but they did not love him. No other people lived at the farm. The old couple owned one cow; that was the extent of their livestock. The cow was named Búkolla.

Once, the cow calved, and the old woman attended to her. When the cow had recovered, the old woman went back to the farmhouse.

A short while later, the old woman returned to check on the cow, but found that it was gone. The old couple searched far and wide, but the cow could not be found.

They were now in a foul temper and ordered their son to go out and search for Búkolla, saying they did not want to see him again unless he had the cow with him. They gave him provisions and a new pair of shoes, and sent him off into the blue yonder.

The boy walked a long, long distance before sitting down to eat something. He then said:

"Let me hear you moo, my Búkolla, if you are still alive."

He then heard the cow moo somewhere far, far away.

Again he walked a long, long distance, and again he sat down to eat, saying: "Let me hear you moo, my Búkolla, if you are still alive."

He then heard Búkolla moo, a little closer than before.

Once more he walked a long, long distance, until he came to some exceedingly tall cliffs. There he sat down to eat, saying, "Let me hear you moo, my Búkolla, if you are still alive."

He then heard the cow mooing beneath his feet. He clambered down the side of the cliffs and saw a very large cave. He entered and saw Búkolla tied beneath a sturdy wooden beam. He untied her immediately, led her out of the cave, and headed for home.

When he had journeyed for a time, he turned to see a large ogre coming after him, and a smaller one with her. He also observed that the large ogre had such a long stride that she would reach him before long.

He then asked: "What do we do now, my Búkolla?"

The cow said: "Take a hair from my tail and lay it on the ground."

He complied. Búkolla then said to the hair: "I pronounce and declare that you shall turn into a mist so large that no one can cross it but the birds in the sky."

At that very instant, the hair was transformed into a huge swath of mist.

When the ogre reached the mist, she cried: "You will not succeed in this, boy! Run home, girl," she ordered the smaller ogre, "and fetch my father's large bull."

The small ogre ran off and presently returned with a very large bull. In an instant, the bull had drunk up all the mist.

The boy then saw that the ogre would reach him in the blink of an eye, for she had such a long stride.

He asked, "What shall we do now, my Búkolla?"

"Take a hair from my tail and lay it on the ground," the cow said.

He complied. Then Búkolla said to the hair: "I pronounce and declare that you shall turn into such a large blazing fire that no one can cross it but the birds in the sky."

In an instant, the hair was transformed into a huge fire.

When the ogre arrived at the fire, she roared: "You will not succeed in this, boy!" She turned to the small ogre: "Go and fetch my father's large bull, girl."

The small ogre ran off, and soon returned with the

bull. It pissed out all the water that it had drunk in with the mist, and thus put out the fire.

The boy then saw that the ogre would reach him in a heartbeat, for she had such a long stride.

He asked, "What can we do now, my Búkolla?"

The cow said: "Take a hair from my tail and lay it on the ground."

He complied. Then Búkolla said to the hair: "I pronounce and declare that you shall turn into such a high mountain that no one can cross it but the birds in the sky."

The hair was instantly transformed into such a tall mountain that the boy saw nothing but the blue sky above.

When the ogre came to the mountain, she thundered: "You will not succeed in this, boy!" To the small ogre she growled: "Fetch my father's large drill, girl."

The small ogre ran off, soon returning with the drill. The large ogre then drilled a hole into the mountain, and the moment she was able to see to the other side she became so eager to get through that she scrambled into the hole. But it was too tight, she became stuck, and finally turned to stone inside the mountain. She remains there to this day.

The boy, on the other hand, found his way home with his Búkolla, much to the delight of the old man and woman.

The Story
of Himinbjörg

O nce upon a time there was a kingdom ruled
by a king and queen. Their names, or the
location of their kingdom, are not known. They had
one son named Sigurður, who was the apple of their
eye. He was a man of exceptional abilities who had
a great affection for his parents and was liked by everyone. Sigurður was a grown man when this story
took place.

It so happened that the queen fell ill, and died. This
was a great tragedy for all, but mostly for the king
and his son. So deep was their grief that they were
unable to find enjoyment in any activity. The wisest
men did their best to console them, and eventually,
through their advice and counsel, the king began to
recover and to enjoy sporting activities once more.

Sigurður, however, continued to grieve for his mother. Nights he would lie at her grave, alone and forlorn, and no man could persuade him to leave. This continued for a time.

One fine day the king and his entourage were taking part in a sporting event at a playing field on the edge of town. Suddenly a bank of clouds appeared. It moved swiftly to the location where the king was playing. A woman then appeared in the clouds and descended to the ground. She was attractive and well attired, and everyone who witnessed this marvelled at her appearance there.

She made her way to where the king was standing and addressed him respectfully. The king returned her greeting amicably and asked her name. She said her name was Himinbjörg, and asked if she could join the court. Many of the king's advisors discouraged him from admitting her, as they were sure that her arrival spelled a great misfortune. But the king found the woman's appearance pleasing. The advisors' discouragement fell on deaf ears, and the king granted her permission to join the court.

Himinbjörg remained in the king's company and soon earned the good favour of the people of the court. Gradually the king developed a deep affection for her, and eventually he announced that he would make her his queen. The announcement was well received, and through the counsel of good men it came to pass that the king and Himinbjörg were wed.

A venerable feast was held to celebrate the wedding, and it was evident that the king had overcome all grief at the death of his former queen. This delighted his people, all but Sigurður, who did not join in the celebrations. He continued to dwell on his mother's passing and to keep vigil by her grave. This was deeply distressing to the king and his associates, yet no one was able to alleviate his grief.

One night, as Sigurður lay on his mother's grave, he was overcome with fatigue. He fell asleep and dreamt that his mother came to him. She appeared angry.

"Here you lie, Sigurður, and in an odd state," said she. "Methinks you waste your time senselessly. You make a spectacle of yourself, lie out here each night like a scoundrel, complaining and lamenting and causing me much grief. This must have consequences. I now declare that you shall have no peace until you have freed a princess who has been turned into a hideous ogre from under that spell."

She then turned away. Sigurður awoke, and thought that he saw her ghost leaving. He went home, took to his bed, and was inconsolable. A host of wise men did their best to assuage his suffering, but to no avail.

The king then asked Himinbjörg if she could

help alleviate Sigurður's pain. She went to him, and through her gentle yet shrewd probing, was able to get him to tell her of his dream, and the reason for his troubles.

She responded by saying that this certainly boded ill, "And it will prove the old adage that there are few things more potent than sorcery. About this curse there is nothing to be done. I have a foster mother," she continued, "and if she cannot help you, I believe that no one can. You must go to her. Take this belt and knife to her as proof that I wish her to help you on your mission. Here is also a ball of yarn. Let it roll in front of you, holding on to one end, and at length it will lead you to the home of my foster mother. I also advise you to be kind to anyone you may encounter along the way. I have a hunch that, after your departure, the court and even your father will turn against me. I shall be blamed for your misfortunes and shall be put to death, unless you come to my rescue."

Thus their conversation ended, and they bid each other a fond farewell.

A short time later Sigurður vanished, and no one knew where he had gone. His loss was keenly felt by all.

Let us now learn of Sigurður's journey. He walked over mountains and through forests, traversing great distances. He felt no hunger on his travels, as Himin-björg had given him a magic sack of provisions, the nature of which was to never become empty. The ball of yarn rolled in front of him, and he followed. Eventually he came to a coastline and began to follow it.

He came upon some cliffs along the coast and saw a large flock of ravens. Counting them, he found there to be fifty in all. They were fighting and tearing at each other over a ledge on the cliff where they all wanted to perch. One raven lay on the ground, evidently very weak. Sigurður found this entire scene very strange and stood a while watching them. Then, remembering his stepmother's advice, he began to hew ledges into the cliffs for all the ravens, subsequently placing each bird on a separate ledge. He placed the weak raven on the ledge over which they had all been fighting. He then gave them food to eat so that they were satiated. As he was leaving, the ravens called out to him, saying that he should summon them if he ever needed help. He replied that he would be glad to be able to call upon them.

Sigurður had but walked a short distance when he saw another cliff with fifty seagulls, in the same predicament as the ravens. He resolved their difficulty in the same way as before.

Coming to a third cliff, he found fifty doves in the same situation as the ravens and seagulls, and settled the matter in the same way as previously. All urged him to summon them if needed, and he responded to their offers with gratitude.

His journey continued without incident, until he arrived at a small farmhouse with a half-open door. There, his ball of yarn came to a halt. Sigurður realized that this was the house to which he had been sent. He knocked at the door, and a very old woman appeared. He asked her name. She responded with indifference, but said that her name was Blákápa. He then asked her for shelter. She did not readily acquiesce, noting that her house was small and that she had not expected guests. "Besides," she added, "I do not know you."

At this, Sigurður conveyed Himinbjörg's greeting to her.

"May the heavens smile upon my foster daughter," she replied. "What news can you give me?"

Sigurður said that he had seen her, "And she has sent me to ask for your assistance."

He then showed her the knife and belt. She examined them and said, "I see by these objects that you speak the truth, and that my foster daughter wishes me to assist you. But first you will stay the night here."

They went inside, where she decked a table for him and served him a meal. When he had eaten his fill she showed him to a bed, where he spent the night in comfort.

The next morning, Blákápa rose early and asked Sigurður about his circumstances. He explained his situation as well as he could, and said why he had come there. Blákápa listened with a concerned expression. Then she said:

"Your troubles are great, Sigurður, no matter how you seek to resolve them. I know the place to which you are being directed. An excellent king reigned a short distance from here. He and his queen had a daughter named Ingigerður, who kept a chamber with eighteen maidens to serve her. All were the daughters of noble men.

"It then happened that the queen died. Soon after that a maiden appeared in the realm and no one knew from whence she had come. She was extremely beautiful, but was in fact a horrible ogre. The king was so enamoured with her beauty that he took her for his queen, and this upset princess Ingigerður greatly. She cared little for her stepmother and therefore became the target of her hostility and wrath. One day the queen went to Ingigerður's chamber and cast a spell on her, ordering that she should turn into a hideous ogre, that all of her handmaidens should become ogres, and that they should kill the king and destroy his kingdom.

"After that she disappeared, and she has not been seen since. Yet her spell was so potent that it all came to pass. The princess and her maidens are all terrifying ogres, and the princess is the worst of all. She has killed her father and her kinsmen and destroyed the kingdom so absolutely that no man can dwell in it. She now resides there with her eighteen servants, and I see that this is the princess to whom you are being sent. You are in grave danger indeed. None who have gone to see her have survived to tell the tale, and unless you are a man of exceptionally good fortune you shall never be able to complete this mission.

"And yet, the spell cast upon you is powerful, and I shall not try to discourage you. I shall do what I can to help you, for that is my foster daughter's wish. Go and call on the fiend today. Make your entrance boldly and sit in the furthest seat. When she enters, answer her questions with confidence. It will do no good to fear them."

Sigurður made his way to the ogre's palace. He had no trouble entering, as the door was open. He followed Blákápa's instructions, and waited for that which would come. Soon he heard a great rumbling outside so that the entire palace trembled. A large and hideous ogre entered, followed by eighteen of the same, all of them fierce in appearance. Never in his life had he seen such horrifying creatures, and the worst one was she who had entered first. She addressed Sigurður irritably, demanding to know who he was and where he was going. He said he hardly knew, that he had chanced upon this place and was thankful for it, as he thought he might rest awhile.

She asked how he might make himself useful. He replied that there was not much he could do.

"If you plan to stay here with us you must do something worthwhile," she replied.

She then walked to the throne and took up a chessboard that was there. It was a splendid item, made from the finest gold. She said: "If you wish to stay here you must earn your keep by fetching another chessboard, in every way as good as this one."

He replied that it would be no easy task, "Or where shall I find it?"

She replied that he would have to discover that on his own, "And remember that your head is at stake if you do not bring me the chessboard before the third sun."

Sigurður went and found Blákápa, telling her what had transpired and about the mission that he was to undertake.

She said: "That is no easy task. The only such

chessboard is owned by two dwarves who prize it highly and guard it zealously. If we are to obtain it we must slay them first. Let us go immediately."

They made their way to the seashore. There Blákápa found a small boat which they rowed until they came to a cliff that rose straight up from the sea. Inside this cliff were the dwarves.

Using her shrewd tricks, Blákápa was able to lure the dwarves out of the cliff, and Sigurður slayed them both. Blákápa found the chessboard and brought it to Sigurður, much to his relief. He carried the chessboard to the ogre's palace and sat down on the furthest seat, as before. On arriving and seeing Sigurður, she said: "There you are, and you will now deliver me the chessboard."

He told her that there was no hope of that, as she had refused to tell him where to find it. At that she scowled, then summoned her cohorts and ordered them to chop him into tiny pieces. They rushed forth to fulfill her order, but at that moment Sigurður brought out the chessboard. The ogre was amazed.

"You have completed this task," she said, "and yet we are not satisfied. To earn your keep you will have to do more."

She then took Sigurður to a castle. Overhead was a glass ceiling supported by four pillars, exquisitely crafted, made of pure gold.

She said: "Here is a glass ceiling held up by four gold pillars. I find the fifth pillar wanting. To earn your keep you must fetch it, and place it here. It must be crafted just like the others, otherwise you shall meet a swift death. You must do this before the third sun."

Sigurður asked her where he should look for the pillar. She replied that he would have to discover that on his own.

He then went to Blákápa and gave her an account of these developments. "There is no end to your troubles," she replied, "and this task is far more difficult than the last."

She told Sigurður that he would find the pillar in a distant palace. Making haste, they arrived at the city in which the palace was located in the evening. Before they encountered anyone Blákápa gave Sigurður a magic stone that would make him invisible. She held on to another one for herself. They entered the city, hiding out in various houses until nightfall. When the city was asleep, they went in search of the pillar. Blákápa led the way, and whenever they came to a locked door she took a wand from her cloak and struck at the door with it, so that it opened. Finally they arrived at the place where the pillar stood, and Blákápa asked Sigurður to try to move it. He tried, but it would not budge.

She then took a pair of gloves from her bag, and put them on. Next she pulled the pillar out from where it stood and placed it on her shoulders, since Sigurður had not the strength to carry it. They then headed homeward, unseen. Blákápa went with Sigurður to the ogre's palace, and with some manoeuvring was able to place the pillar where the ogre had instructed. She then went home, while Sigurður waited.

When the ogre arrived, a similar scene took place as with the chessboard.

The ogre said: "It is odd how much you can do, being so young, and I am certain that you are not alone in this game. I have ordered many men to perform this task, and none have succeeded. Yet you shall have to do more if you want to stay alive and be left in peace. I have an ox in the forest which you must slaughter in a day. No one may assist you. You must spill its blood on my tablecloth, then wash the tablecloth and return it to me white as snow. You must knead the hide, and return it to me as soft as wool. You must polish the horns, and return them to me as shiny as gold. All this you must do before the third sun. Your head is at stake."

Sigurður left, found Blákápa, and told her what had transpired.

On hearing this, Blákápa became deeply distressed, saying: "You will now almost certainly die. This ox of which the ogre speaks is a terrible beast, and it will most likely swallow you whole. It grieves me that I cannot save you. I shall help you create a strategy, but I must not go with you. Look for the ox, and when you find it, lay down the tablecloth." She handed him a small sack containing a powder-like substance. "Spread this on the cloth, and if the ox sniffs at it you must immediately jump onto its back and stab it with a knife to the heart, near the shoulder blade. Hold on no matter where it runs, until it falls down dead. You will have to hold on tight, and even if you manage it there is great risk involved. Now go, and may good fortune be with you."

Sigurður thanked her, and went on his way. He carried out everything according to her instructions, and with great difficulty managed to slay the ox. He skinned it and removed the horns, then sat down to rest, as he was very weary.

At that point he began to think about how he might perform the other tasks that the ogre had ordered. He saw no way of doing so, and was certain of his own imminent death.

He then thought out loud, speaking these words: "If ever there was a time that I needed my ravens, my seagulls and my doves, this is it."

In that instant he observed a vast number of birds approaching. They were his birds, in three separate flocks. One flock took the tablecloth, the other the hide, and the third the horns. Then they flew away. Sigurður went home to Blákápa and told her of all that had taken place. She rejoiced at his news, and they slept soundly through the night.

The next morning, they found all the objects that the birds had taken in front of Blákápa's door, delivered exactly in the condition that the ogre had ordered they should be.

Blákápa handed the objects to Sigurður. "Take these to the ogre today. She will no doubt be startled when she sees them." She handed him a horn with liquid inside. "If you see her appearance changing, pour some of this on her. Do the same with the others. After that, you can leave with the one you choose."

Sigurður went to the palace and, as before, waited for the ogre to arrive. When she entered she looked so grotesque that Sigurður could hardly bear to lay eyes on her. She demanded to know what had transpired. He replied that the task she had assigned him had been impossible to carry out, as it would have been for anyone. On hearing this, she flew into a rage and shouted for the other ogresses to chop him into pieces. They rushed outside and swiftly returned with their axes.

At this, Sigurður brought out the objects and showed them to the ogress. All at once a great calm came over her, and she lost consciousness, as did the others. The ogre guises fell away, revealing them all to be lovely maidens.

Sigurður acted quickly. Outside the palace door he lit a large fire, then gathered up the ogre guises and threw them into the flames where they quickly turned to ashes. Next he took out the horn and dripped its contents on each of the maidens. Slowly they awakened, and began to take nourishment.

Then Ingigerður spoke. "Who is this man that has so greatly assisted us?"

Sigurður told her his name and who his people were.

She said: "You have done us an enormous service, one from which I benefit the most. I shall never be able to fully repay it. Choose your reward; I shall not refuse you."

He praised her for the gesture, and said that he wished to take her for his wife. She said she would make good on her promise, "But first I think you should go and find your father to let him know what has become of you. Surely he and your friends will be sick with concern."

Sigurður agreed, and began arranging his trip home. It was decided that Ingigerður would wait for his return.

Let us now return to the point in the story when Sigurður vanished. All went as Himinbjörg had foreseen. She was held responsible for his disappearance, and was sentenced to death. Yet the king gave her a three-year period of grace, should there be any news of him. If there was not, she was to be burned to death.

And now, as it happened, everything came together at once: the fire was lit, Himinbjörg was led to it, and Sigurður arrived home.

Everyone was stunned and amazed to see him return, and a momentous feast ensued. Sigurður told of his travels, and Himinbjörg announced that she had, in fact, arranged all so that he would free Ingigerður from the spell, for Ingigerður was her sister. The birds that Sigurður had saved were their relatives, and they had also been under a spell. Much jubilation ensued, ale was drunk in celebration, and Sigurður and the king set off with a vast entourage to fetch Ingigerður.Himinbjörg joined them, and Sigurður wed Ingigerður in the presence of all his kin. They settled down in the kingdom and loved one another very much, enjoying much prosperity and good fortune. Among their descendants are numerous chieftains and dignitaries, which shall not be listed here. And thus ends this story.

Note: *The name Himinbjörg, literally translated, means "saviour from the sky," or "heavenly saviour."*

ABOUT THE TRANSLATOR

Alda Sigmundsdóttir is a writer, journalist and translator. She was born in Iceland, raised in Canada, and has also lived in Germany, Cyprus and the United Kingdom. She has written extensively about Iceland for the international media and regularly gives talks and lectures about various aspects of Icelandic society. Catch up with Alda on her website aldasigmunds.com, or find her on Facebook, Twitter and Instagram.

Other books by Alda Sigmundsdóttir, available through Amazon or on aldasigmunds.com:

The Little Book of Tourists in Iceland
The Little Book of Icelandic
The Little Book of the Icelanders
The Little Book of the Icelanders in the Old Days
The Little Book of the Hidden People
Unraveled - a Novel About a Meltdown
Living Inside the Meltdown

ACKNOWLEDGEMENTS

I am deeply indebted to five people who helped me with this project.

First of all, to the four people who volunteered to be beta readers, and as such provided invaluable comments and insights: Bill Crandall, Giacomo Giudici, Paul Hutchinson and Ted Wenskus. Extra special thanks to my husband, Erlingur Páll Ingvarsson, who designed this book, and whose unfailing help and dedication to this project (including working through a particularly nasty bout of flu) was invaluable. Huge thanks also to the many followers of my Facebook page and blog who got in touch and volunteered to read for me – you rock!

ICELANDIC FOLK LEGENDS

© Sigmundsdóttir

4th Edition

Little Books Publishing

Reykjavík, 2016

Layout and cover design: Erlingur Páll Ingvarsson

The pattern on the cover of this book and the ornaments distributed
throughout are traditional Icelandic designs, taken from the book
Íslensk sjónabók - Ornaments and Patterns found in Iceland.

Printing: Prentmidlun Ltd., Poland

ISBN 978-1-970125-05-4

LITTLE BOOKS
PUBLISHING

Printed in Poland
by Amazon Fulfillment
Poland Sp. z o.o., Wrocław